PURPLE COWS
&
POTATO CHIPS

Language Acquisition Activities
for Sensory Learning Styles

PHOTOCOPIABLE LESSONS FOR GRADES
FIVE THROUGH ADULT

Mary Ann Christison
University of Utah

Sharron Bassano
University of California Extension

Alta Book Center Publishers
San Francisco, California 94010 USA
Email: info@altaesl.com
Website: www.altaesl.com

Project Editor: Helen Munch
Copy Editor: Carol Ann Brimeyer
Production/Design: E. Carol Gee
Illustrations: Kathleen B. Peterson
Cover Art: Helen Daniels
Compositors: Arlene Hardwick/Elizabeth L. Tong

ALTA BOOK CENTER PUBLISHERS–SAN FRANCISCO
14 Adrian Court
Burlingame, California 94010 USA
Phone: 800 ALTA/ESL • 650.692.1285
Fax: 800 ALTA/FAX • 650.692.4654
Email: info@altaesl.com
Website: www.altaesl.com

Printed in the United States of America

ISBN 1-882483-31-6
ISBN 978-1882483-31-0

DEDICATION

This book is dedicated to our students for providing the inspiration for the activities; to the many teachers in workshops and in-service training sessions for their comments and ideas for improving the material; and to our editor, Helen Munch, for her suggestions on organizing and further refining the manuscript.

CONTENTS

UNIT 1: PURPLE COWS
Sight

UNIT 2: WET LEAVES
Touch/Movement

UNIT 3: THUNDERSTORMS
Hearing

UNIT 4: POTATO CHIPS
Smell/Taste

Introduction

About This Book

Purple Cows & Potato Chips is a resource book for language teachers in grades five through adult and in university intensive programs. It features 56 stimulating, non-traditional activities designed to promote language acquisition through exploration of the primary senses. *Unit 1: Purple Cows* focuses on the sense of sight; *Unit 2: Wet Leaves* examines touch and movement; *Unit 3: Thunderstorms* deals with the sense of hearing; and *Unit 4: Potato Chips* explores the senses of smell and taste. Each unit begins with specific Notes to the Teacher on how to prepare for and present each of the activities in that unit, followed by 14 duplicatable exercise sheets.

About The Activities

We believe that in order to become more fluent in English, students need more quality listening time, more active participation, more self-investment in the language, and less stress. They need to use their second language skills in a coherent context and in interactive settings.

The activities in *Purple Cows & Potato Chips* are designed to provide students with opportunities to expand their communication skills through individual, pair, and coorperative group work. Since the activities are self-contained, they can be used in any order, allowing you to match them to both the interests and needs of your students.

Participation in these multi-sensory activities will allow your students to perceive language acquisition as a pleasant and enjoyable experience involving the whole self.

How To Use This Book

To ensure the success of both the initial and subsequent activities, we recommend that you read the following general suggestions for preparing for, presenting, and wrapping-up the activities.

Preparation

- Read the **Notes to the Teacher** for the activity you have chosen. The notes begin each unit and tell what materials you need (if any), how to make the activity work smoothly, and what to do when the activity is completed.

- Assemble the materials needed and prepare student copies of the appropriate duplicatable exercise sheet.

- Divide the class into pairs or small groups, as necessary.

Presentation

- Explain to your students what they will be doing and how it will help them become better speakers of English. Provide plenty of explanation and clarification, and check often for student comprehension. Students must understand what you are saying in order to participate in the activities and improve their English skills.

- Distribute copies of the exercise sheet.

- Read the directions aloud, or have students read them silently. Clarify any difficult vocabulary and make sure that students understand the directions and what is expected of them.

- If the activity requires group work, make sure students know what group they are in, who the other members are, and what each member is to do when. (Some activities will ask that one group member be timekeeper or scorekeeper.) An activity may begin with students working alone or with a partner, and then forming groups. Or, you may initiate an activity with the entire class before dividing students into groups.

- Give students a time limit for each activity so they know how quickly they must work.

NOTE: Occasionally, you may want to invite native English speakers to visit your class to join your groups as participants. Visitors need not have teaching or tutoring experience. Their presence in class provides potential for native speaker input and additional group participation. Classroom visitors might be from volunteer bureaus, senior citizen organizations, retired persons associations, the YMCA/YWCA, bilingual and international programs at local churches or schools, or elsewhere.

Wrap Up

- In most cases, you will want to reconvene students at the end of the class period to discuss individual or group results. Did students enjoy the activity? Was it easy? Difficult? Why? What part was the best or the most fun? Were there any problems? What could be done to solve the problems?

- If the activity requires clean up, leave enough time for students to participate too!

Orientation Activity

The orientation activity, Expanding Your Senses (p viii), is intended to familiarize you and your students with the book's underlying theme: language acquisition through multi-sensory activities. We recommend that you introduce this activity first, before beginning any one of the four units.

Students in our language classes have been doing these multi-sensory activities for many years with fun and success. We are delighted to share the activities and hope that you enjoy them as much as we do.

Mary Ann Christison
Sharron Bassano

Notes to the Teacher

Expanding Your Senses

This orientation activity should help students become more aware of sensory involvement in the language acquisition process. This involvement may be demonstrated by exaggerating the functions our senses perform.

Begin by explaining that our senses can deceive us. For example, an object far away appears smaller in size than the same object close by. The size of the object doesn't change as we approach it; our perception of the object changes. Point out the use of the word "feel" to refer to the sense of touch as opposed to an emotional response. Give an example like "The cat feels furry" and "The cat feels sad."

After distributing the exercise sheets, answer the first one or two questions with the class, gathering as many ideas and responses as you can. Then have students work with partners to complete the exercise sheet. Finish up with a large group sharing of answers at the end of class.

Expanding Your Senses

Directions: *Work with a partner.* Write a one-word answer to each question. Then explain your answer to your partner. When you finish, *share your answers with the class.*

1. What does the wind taste like?_____

2. What does sadness look like? _____

3. What does green smell like? _____

4. What does blue sound like? _____

5. What does music feel like?_____

6. What does an apple sound like? _____

7. What does love look like?_____

8. What does the moon smell like?_____

9. What does Friday feel like? _____

10. What does a sigh look like? _____

11. What does yellow sound like? _____

12. What does black taste like? _____

PURPLE COWS

Unit 1
Notes to the Teacher

1.1 Making Improvements

The illustrations should make vocabulary problems minimal; however, check for understanding if you have a low level class and/or your students are unfamiliar with western culture. The key to this activity is understanding the concept of improvement. Use the first two items on the list as examples. Give one idea for an improvement and write it on the board. For example, a *television* might be better if it allowed you to talk back to it or if it showed only those programs you wanted to see. Ask for and write down other ideas from all students in the class. Accept each response as given, as long as it conveys understanding of the concept of improvement. Then ask students to work in small groups to complete the activity. A large group sharing at the end, with notes written on the board, is an excellent wrap-up.

1.2 Picture Words and Word Pictures

Introduce this activity by explaining that we generally express our thoughts in writing by means of words *or* pictures. It is possible, however, to communicate an idea by combining both words *and* pictures in an interesting way. In the first part of this activity, students "read" (decipher) Picture Words (p. 8), describing the makeup of each word, the position and function of its individual letters.

When students have completed their exercise sheets, have them reconvene as a class to share their answers to Picture Words. First identify the words, then ask students questions such as:

What letter makes up the fin of the shark...?
What letters make up the ears of the kangaroo...?
What do the *O's* represent on the kangaroo...?
What do the *S's* represent on the mouse...?
What letter makes up the trunk of the elephant...?
What letters make up the sail of the boat...?
What letter makes up the flag on the boat...?

In the second part of the activity, students work with partners to create their own Word Pictures (p. 9). A good way to end is by having volunteers draw their pictures on the board.

1.3 What Do You See?

This activity demonstrates that people don't always see things exactly the same way. Begin the activity with the class, looking at Figure 1. Students should be able to see two different patterns (a vase and facing profiles). Ask students to explain in what ways the patterns are different. Then have students work with partners on Figures 2 to 6, sharing their answers at the end of class.

1.4 What Can We Do?

Begin this activity by brainstorming with the class over one item on the list (or one you think up). Try to elicit as many different ideas as possible. The first few will usually be ordinary and obvious, but later suggestions should prove more creative and unusual. For example, here is one group's list of uses for a wooden spoon: stir soup; dig in the garden; taste cake batter; push the clothes down in the washing machine; prop open a window; play in the sand; point to something; paddle a small boat; get something from under the refrigerator; and swat flies. Let students work in small groups, then follow up with a large group sharing.

1.5 Taking Shapes

Before distributing the exercise sheets, draw the following figure on the board:

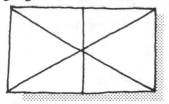

Ask the class what different shapes and combinations of shapes students can identify in it. There are a number of possible answers as follows:

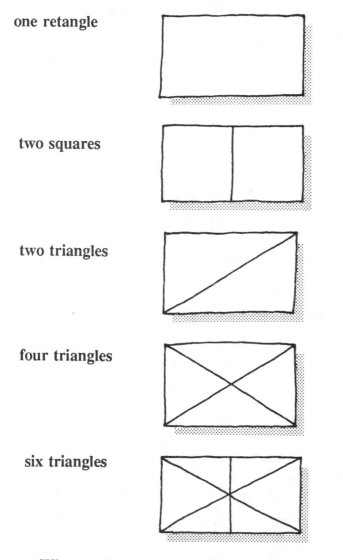

one retangle

two squares

two triangles

four triangles

six triangles

When students have identified at least the five basic shapes above, erase the figure and have one student, from memory, describe one of the shapes or combinations to a partner. Then have students work in small groups to complete the exercise sheet.

1.6 Silly Inventions

Begin this activity with a five- to ten-minute group discussion of the question "What do you need help with in your life?" Then have students work in groups. Stress that the machine they invent should do things that can help them in their own lives.

1.7 Advertising

For this activity you will need to bring a variety of old magazines to class. (Flea markets, supermarkets, libraries, medical offices, and neighbors are good magazine sources.) Preview the magazines for a wide selection of the advertisements described on the students' list. Work together as a class on one or two ads before students form groups. We have found that awarding a prize to the winning team adds fun to this activity.

1.8 Similar Symbols

Begin by having all the students classify the symbols into as many different groups as possible. Put several symbols on the board and ask students to tell you what these symbols have in common. For example, symbols 1, 4, 6, 7, and 9 all contain circles within them: symbols 2, 5, 11, and 15 all contain triangles, and so on. Give the class ten minutes to create as many ways as possible to group the symbols. Then have students work with partners.

1.9 What Comes Next?

This is a particularly challenging activity that evokes a lot of discussion. After distributing the exercise sheets, do Sequence 1 as an example. Here are some solutions for the other sequences (There may be more than one correct solution in some cases):

Two additional barbells get blackened in each figure.

Sequence 1

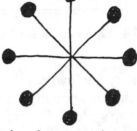

The double triangles rotate 1 space to the right in each figure.

Sequence 2

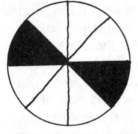

Moving L to R from the top left, 3 blank squares separate the black squares in each figure.

Sequence 3

One end of the diagonal barbell pointing R alternates with the other end in getting blackened.

Sequence 4

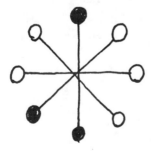

Moving L to R from the top left, the blank squares separating the black squares increase by 1.

Sequence 5

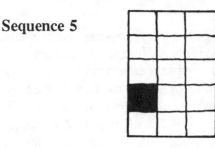

The triangle directly opposite the blackened triangle in the preceding figure gets blackened.

Sequence 6

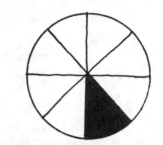

Moving ten spaces from the last blackened triangle, the next triangle gets blackened.

Sequence 7

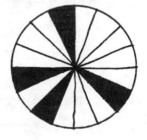

Sequence 8

Encourage students to create their own incomplete sequences for others in the class to complete.

1.10 Cartoon Sequencing

For this activity, each group can use the same cartoon sequence or different sequences. The pictures are not sequenced correctly. Students must first decide on a sequence and number the pictures 1, 2, and 3 *before* they write their dialogs on a separate sheet of paper. As students work, circulate among them to ask and answer questions and offer suggestions. Allow time for the groups to practice their dialogs before they present them to the class.

1.11 Ink Designs

Give students ten minutes to brainstorm about the things they see in the ink designs. Stress the ability to explain as well as *locate* what they see. Follow up with a group sharing to see how many different things students were able to find in the designs.

1.12 Incomplete Pictures

The ability to build on incomplete information is a skill needed by all language learners. This activity provides practice in building on visual information. Have students work alone and share their finished pictures with the class.

1.13 Memory Pictures

Ask each group to appoint a recorder who will be sent briefly out of the room. Then distribute copies of the exercise sheet (p. 27), one sheet per group. Make certain that the sheets are folded so that only the Directions are showing.

Review the exercise directions with the students in the class. Explain that students will have one minute, after you say "Go!", to study the picture in hand; when you say "Stop!", the recorders will return to class and students will have ten minutes to tell them about the picture. Group members can help their recorders with spelling only. Complete sentences are unnecessary. At the end of the time limit, ask the groups to check for specific things on their list. The group with the most accurate and complete list of items, wins.

1.14 U.S.A., Here I Come!

This activity has two parts. For the first part, ask each group to appoint a secretary to write down the group's ideas. Distribute copies of the first exercise sheet (p. 28), one per group, and review the directions. Tell students that they will have eight minutes to record their ideas. Any idea is acceptable, be it funny, serious, even crazy. At the end of the time period, ask one group to share its ideas with the class. Write the ideas on the board and encourage students to add their own reasons for coming to the U.S.A.

For the second part of the activity repeat the procedure using the second exercise sheet (p. 29), and follow up with a group sharing of personal experiences. In both cases, the group with the most ideas wins.

1.1 Making Improvements

Directions: *Work with a small group (3 to 5 students).* Read the words on the list below and think of different ways to improve the items. Be creative! There are no limits. Have one person write down the group's ideas for each item. *Share your answers with the class.*

1. Television

2. Alarm clock

3. Radio

4. Pen

5. Computer

6. Refrigerator

7. Toaster

8. Hair dryer

9. Can opener

10. Bicycle

1.2 Picture Words and Word Pictures

Directions: *Work with a partner.* Look at the pictures on this page. Identify the word that makes up each picture and the individual letters of that word. Write the word below each picture.

1. _____

2. _____

3. _____

4. _____

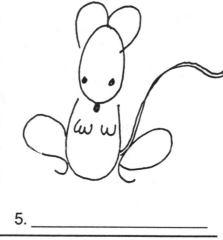

5. _____

6. _____

7. _____

Continued

Now look at this list of words. Draw pictures using the letters of each word. Begin with words that seem easy to work with. *Show your picture words to the class.*

1. C A T

2. R A D I O

3. P H O N E

4. C A S H

5. H O L E

6. F U N

7. S I X

8. C U P

1.3 What Do You See?

Directions: *Work with a partner.* Look at the figures below and on page 11. You should be able to see two different patterns in each figure. (If you have trouble, turn the pages upside down or sideways.) Discuss the figures with your partner. Try to describe everything you see. Can you explain the differences in the patterns? Which pattern is easier for you to see? *Share your ideas with the class.*

Figure 1

Figure 2

Figure 3

Figure 4

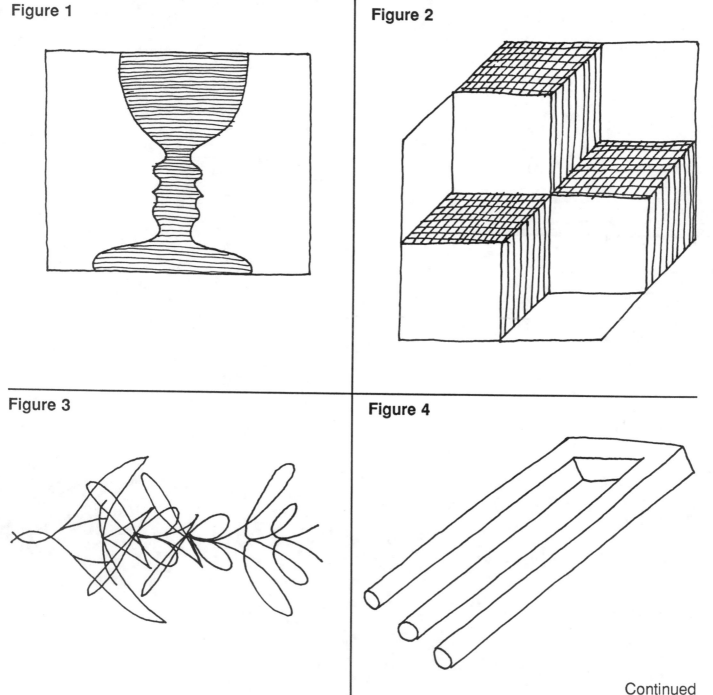

Purple Cows & Potato Chips ©1995 by Alta Book Center Publishers Permission is granted to reproduce this page for classroom use.

Continued

Figure 5

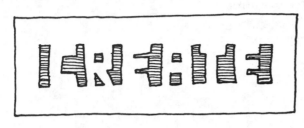

Figure 6

1.4 What Can We Do?

Directions: *Work with a small group (3 to 5 students). Look at the words and pictures below and list all the different things you can think of to do with each item. Share your answers with the class.*

1. Hammer _____

   _____

2. Clothes dryer _____

   _____

3. Garden hose _____

   _____

4. Vacuum cleaner _____

   _____

5. Calendar _____

   _____

6. Newspaper _____

   _____

7. Hairbrush _____

   _____

8. Rock _____

   _____

9. Rope _____

   _____

10. Large wooden spoon _____

    _____

1.5 Taking Shapes

Directions: *Work with a small group (3 to 5 students).* Look
at the figures below. Try dividing them into as many
combinations as possible. *Explain your combinations
to the class.*

Figure 1

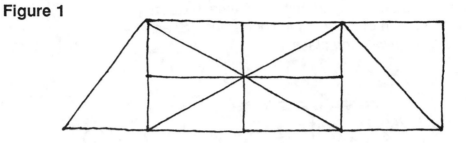

Figure 2

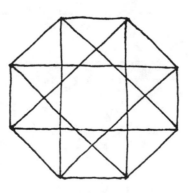

Figure 3

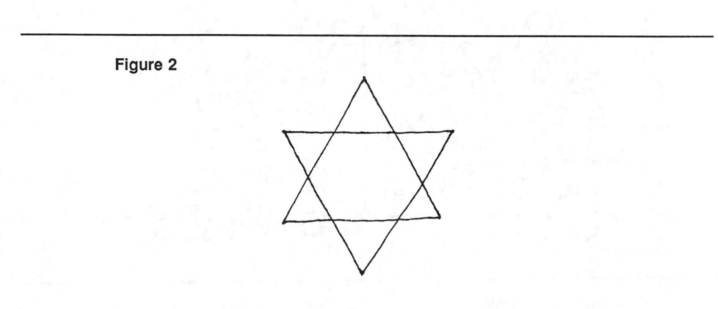

1.6 Silly Inventions

Directions: *Work with a small group (3 to 5 students).* Look at the picture below. It is a machine that can do anything you want. With your classmates, decide on *five* things you want this machine to do to help you in your life. Remember, the machine can do *anything* you want, and it can do more than one thing at a time. Explain exactly which part of the machine does what. *Share your information with the class.*

Part of the machine	What it does
1.	
2.	
3.	
4.	
5.	

1.7 Advertising

Directions: *Work with a small group (3 to 5 students).* Your teacher will give you some magazines. Look at the words listed below and try to find magazine ads for as many of the items as possible. As soon as you find an appropriate ad, tear it out, number it according to the list, and cross the item off the list. Work as quickly as you can and see how many *different* ads you can find. Read the ads carefully. The group with the greatest number of different ads wins. *Share your advertisements with the class.*

Find an ad for:

1.	Toothpaste		11.	A soft drink
2.	Dishwasher soap		12.	Candy
3.	Cat food		13.	A stereo
4.	Dog food		14.	Women's perfume
5.	Cereal		15.	A TV
6.	Hand soap		16.	A computer
7.	Oven cleaner		17.	A DVD player
8.	Insurance		18.	A car
9.	Mouthwash		19.	Men's clothes
10.	Some kind of medicine		20.	A camera

1.8 Similar Symbols

Directions: *Work with a partner.* Look at the symbols below and classify them in as many different ways as you can. Put as many symbols as possible in each group.

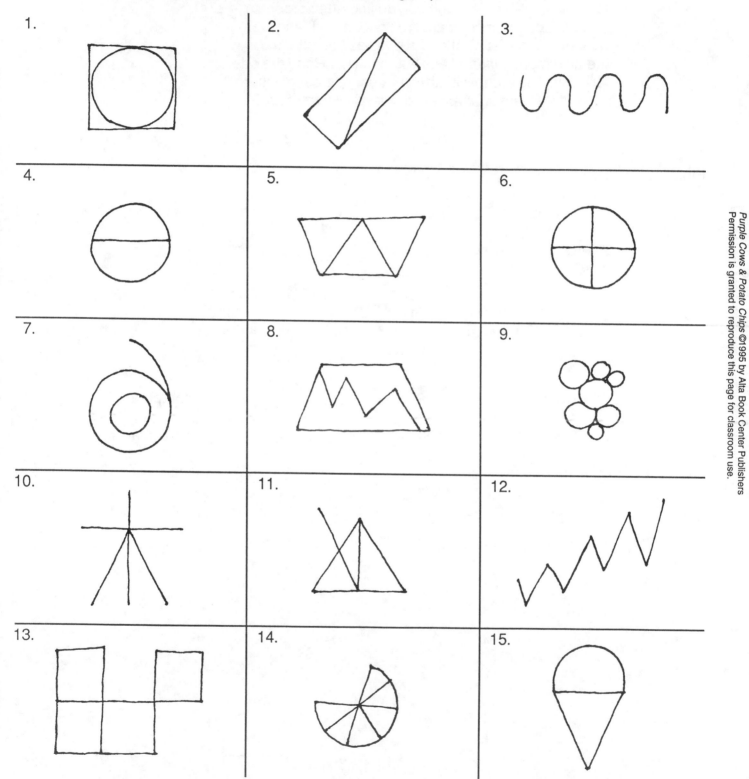

1.

2.

3.

4.

5.

6.

7.

8.

9.

10.

11.

12.

13.

14.

15.

Purple Cows & Potato Chips ©1995 by Alta Book Center Publishers Permission is granted to reproduce this page for classroom use.

1.9 What Comes Next?

Directions: *Work alone.* Look at the sequences of figures below and on page 18. Try to determine how each sequence is arranged. Study each figure to see why **B** follows **A** and **C** follows **B**. Then complete figure **D**. *Share your answers with the class.*

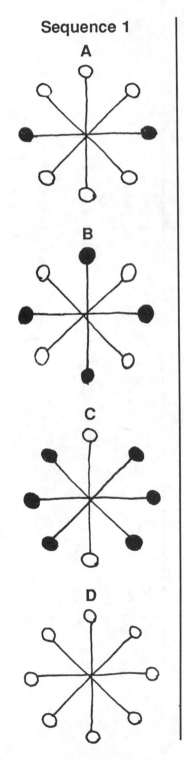

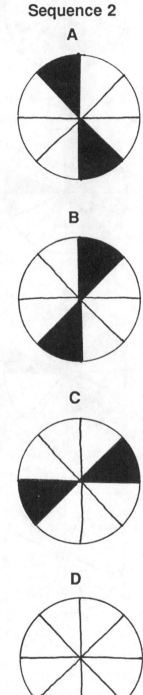

Sequence 1
A
B
C
D

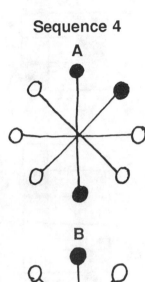
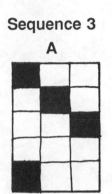

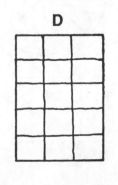

Sequence 2
A
B
C
D

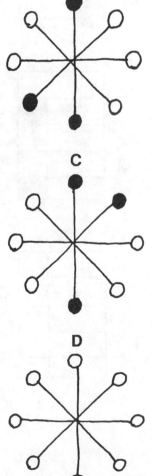

Sequence 3
A
B
C
D

Sequence 4
A
B
C
D

Continued

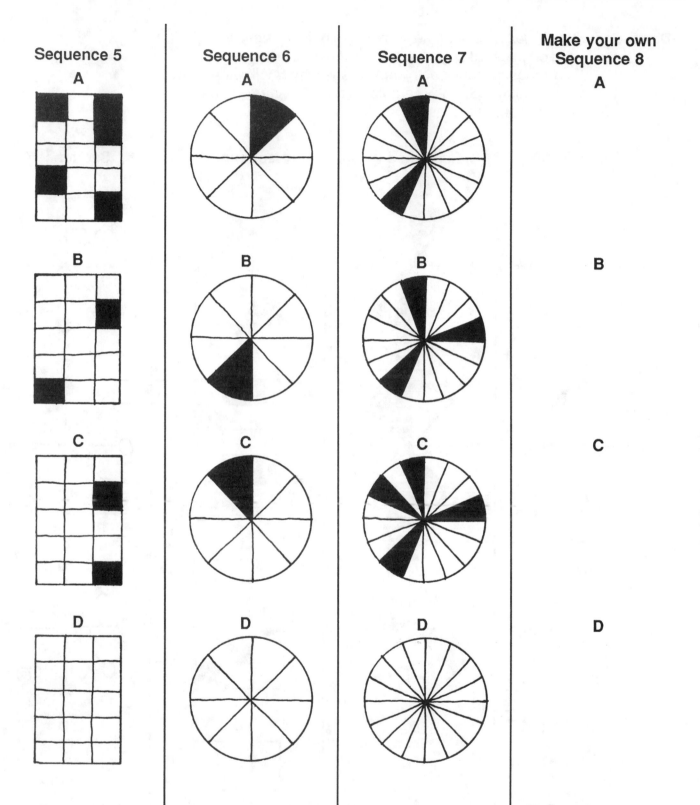

Sequence 5   Sequence 6   Sequence 7   **Make your own Sequence 8**

A   A   A   A

B   B   B   B

C   C   C   C

D   D   D   D

Purple Cows & Potato Chips ©1995 by Alta Book Center Publishers
Permission is granted to reproduce this page for classroom use.

1.10 Cartoon Sequencing

Directions: *Work with a small group (3 to 5 students).* Look at the pictures below and on page 20. Decide on a story sequence and number the pictures 1, 2, and 3. Then, on a separate sheet of paper, write a short dialog telling what the characters are saying to each other. *Share your dialog with the class.*

Sequence 1

_____ _____ _____

Sequence 2

_____ _____ _____

Continued

Sequence 3

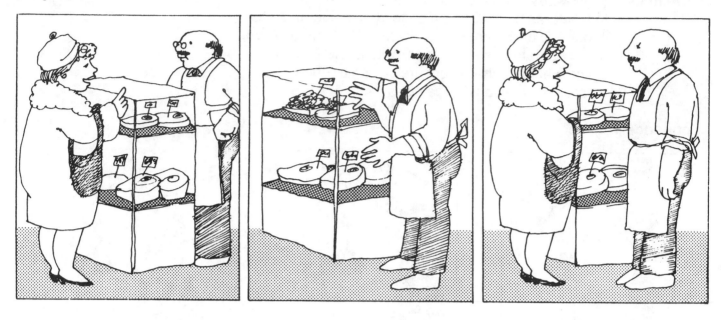

Sequence 4

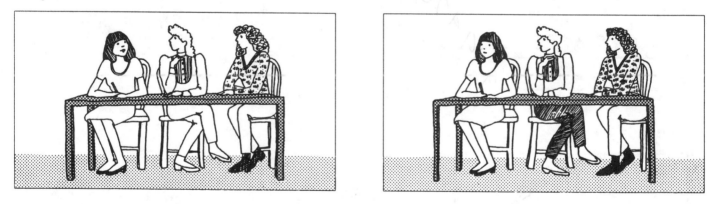

1.11 Ink Designs

Directions: *Work with a partner or a small group (3 to 4 students). Study the ink designs below and on page 22. Find five different things in each design. Be prepared to explain to the class what you see and where it is.*

Ink Design 1

What do you see?

1. _____

2. _____

3. _____

4. _____

5. _____

Continued

Ink Design 2

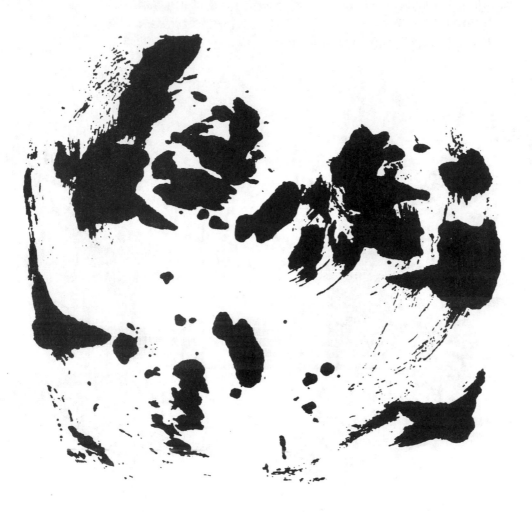

What do you see?

1. _____

2. _____

3. _____

4. _____

5. _____

1.12 Incomplete Pictures

Directions: *Work alone.* Look at the pictures below and on pages 24, 25, and 26. Decide how to complete each picture and draw in the missing lines. *Share your pictures with the class* and explain what each one is or represents.

Continued

1.13 Memory Pictures

Directions: *Work with a small group (3 to 4 students).* When your
teacher says "Go!", unfold this exercise sheet and
look closely at the picture. Try to remember everything
you see in it. (Don't write anything down!) When your
teacher says "Stop!", refold the exercise sheet and tell
your group's "recorder" everything you recall seeing
in the picture. *Share your answers with the class.*

1.14 U.S.A., Here I Come!

Directions: *Work with a small group (3 to 4 students).* Look at the picture below of a "new arrival" to the United States. Help your group's "secretary" make a list of all the possible reasons why this person came to the U.S.A. Try to get at least ten ideas. *Share your list with the class.*

Purple Cows & Potato Chips ©1995 by Alta Book Center Publishers
Permission is granted to reproduce this page for classroom use.

Continued

Now look at this picture of a person who has been in the U.S.A.
a few months. Make a list of all the possible problems this newcomer
might be facing. *Share your list with the class.*

Unit 2

WET LEAVES

Notes to the Teacher

2.1 Dice Games

We have found dice games to be very useful in helping students develop their language as well as computation and problem-solving skills. For this activity you will need to bring enough pairs of dice to class for several student groups. Emphasize individual work for computation; group work should be for checking. Resolve any differences in group totals when the class reconvenes.

2.2 Card Games

Card games also help students develop language, computation, and problem-solving skills. Be sure to bring enough decks of playing cards for several student groups. Before beginning the activity, review the cards in the deck and the scoring key with the class. As in "Dice Games," emphasize individual work first, followed by partner and group work for checking answers.

2.3 Feeling Bags

For this activity you will need six or seven large paper bags, each containing several different objects. (Make certain the objects are not sharp or dangerous.) Demonstrate the activity first before having students work in small groups. Let each group select a bag, then have the groups rotate the bags often to keep the guessing lively. Stress that as individual students describe the objects, their classmates should be writing down their words.

2.4 Picture Stories

For this activity you will need several old magazines or catalogs, scissors, glue, and construction paper. The activity takes two class periods: one for students to find, cut out, glue the pictures, and write their stories; another for students to share their stories with the class. We usually begin by demonstrating the procedure with a story we have made. Include some sample pre-listening questions such as: "Is this a story about an airplane or a scuba diver?... Are these people going fishing or diving?..." Use Yes/No or Either/Or questions and write students' answers on the board.

2.5 Charades

Adjectives, nouns, or other words are additional possibilities for this activity. A prize for the winning group adds a nice touch.

2.6 Body Language

Before you present this activity, review the actions described on the exercise sheet to make certain you understand them. Practice each action so you can repeat it several times for the students. After demonstrating an action, allow student pairs plenty of time to write down the meaning and think of a sentence.

2.7 Simon Says

Before distributing the exercise sheet, write the sample commands on the board. Then demonstrate the commands and distribute the exercise sheets. Give students five minutes to write other commands they can use when they are the "leader." Circulate among the groups, suggesting alternatives to the commands listed on the board. Such suggestions offer opportunities for vocabulary development.

2.8 May I?

Before doing this activity, you will need to clear desks and chairs from the middle of the room. Then have students line up across the back of the room. Explain that the object of the activity is to reach the front of the room. To do so, students will have to answer questions and perform simple actions correctly. If a student's answer is correct, s/he may then move by asking "May I...?" before describing the movement. (Example: "May I take a step?") If a student fails to ask "May I...?" or uses his/her native language, the student must return to the back of the room.

Begin by asking students these six questions:
1. What are three states in the U.S. that begin with the letter "M"?
2. Who was the first U.S. President?
3. How many states are in the United States?
4. Who are three students in our class?
5. What are the names of three well-known world leaders?
6. Look at the student next to you. Is he or she from your own native country? If *yes*, shake his or her hand. If *no*, do nothing.

Then have students brainstorm at least 12 more questions they can use if they become "leader." Circulate and check questions and offer ideas. Stress that questions should be general ones that most students could answer or would have information about from class.

2.9 Origami

For this activity you will need approximately five sheets of paper for each student and multiple copies of the exercise sheets (pp. 47–53). Cutting the paper into squares can be a class project. It will take two class periods to complete both the oral and written work for this activity.

Explain to students that they will be working with the special art of paper-folding called *origami*. If you have students who are Japanese or who are familiar with the art, be sure to enlist them in your demonstration, as the procedure is somewhat complicated. Be certain you explain very carefully what you want students to do. You may find it easier to assign patterns to group members rather than have them each select one. As students work, circulate among the groups answering questions and offering suggestions. After one student in each group has completed a figure, suggest that the student practice making that figure again so s/he can explain the procedure to the others in the group.

2.10 Money Game

For this activity you will need to bring newspaper advertisements and catalogs to class. Include practical houseware advertisements and clothing. Partners should work together on *one* exercise sheet.

2.11 Aerobics

As students perform this activity, circulate among different pairs. Encourage students to repeat the directions in order to correct misunderstandings, as they work through the exercise.

2.12 Sentence Starters

Students need to walk around for this activity. Stress the importance of getting to know each other's names. Students must work with a different person for each statement. Follow up with a large group sharing. Ask questions such as "How many different favorite foods are there?... Who has the same favorite food?... What things would you buy with $500?... What is the most difficult thing about English?" You may want to write the different answers on the board.

2.13 Perfect Match

Distribute copies of the exercise sheet (p. 57) and explain vocabulary as necessary. Allow students five minutes to mark their answers. Then review each statement one by one, asking students to stand in different corners of the room according to the answer they marked (a's in one corner, b's in a second corner, and so on.)

As you proceed through the statements, encourage comments and discussion. Ask questions such as "Is this something you've done and liked?" or "Is this something you haven't done and would like to do?" Suggest that students get together outside of class to pursue some of their common interests. Notice if the make-up of the groups shifts or remains constant from answer to answer and whose likes are similar or very different.

2.14 Preference Grids

For this activity you will need to make copies of both exercise sheets (pp. 58 and 59). You will also need several pairs of scissors.

Distribute one copy of each exercise sheet per student and review the directions. For p. 59 you might want to suggest some activities to get students started, such as *rollerskate, crochet, paint, play soccer,* and so on. Emphasize that students can move their "preference squares" around on their grids and erase/substitute answers while other students are still responding to your question. Have students share their grids with one another and do a large group sharing to find out what answers were the most and least popular, and why.

2.1 Dice Games

Directions: *Work with a small group* (3 to 5 students), but complete each exercise alone. Your teacher will give you dice. Write your answers in the squares. Check your answers with those of your group members. Do you all have the same totals? *Explain your group's answers to the class.*

Dice Game A

1. Roll the dice *five* times, taking turns with your group members. Write the total of each roll in the boxes a, b, c, d, and e below.

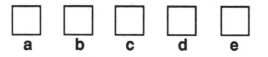

   a   b   c   d   e

2. Multiply **b** by **e**.

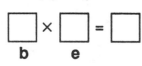

   b   e

3. Add **c** to your answer in *2*.

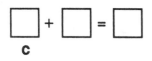

   c

4. Divide the total in *3*. by itself.

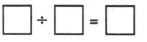

5. Add **d** plus 10 to your answer in *4*.

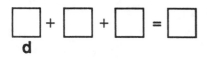

   d

6. Subtract **a** from your total in *5*.

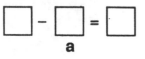

      a

7. Your final answer is: _____ .

Continued

Dice Game B

1. Roll the dice once. Add the two numbers and write the total in the boxes below.

2. Roll the dice again. Add the two numbers and subtract 2 from that total. Add the remainder to the total in *1*.

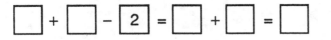

3. Add 7 to the total in *2*.

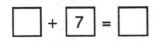

4. Multiply the total in *3*. by 2.

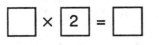

5. Roll the dice again. If you roll a double 6 or a double 2, divide your answer in *4*. by 2. If you roll anything else, do nothing.

6. Roll again. If the total on your dice is over 6, add 20 to your answer in *4*.

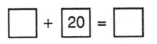

7. Your final answer is: _____ .

2.2 Card Games

Directions: *Work with a partner.* Your teacher will bring playing cards to class. With your partner, complete the steps below. Check your answer and *be prepared to explain it to the class.*

Card Game A
Scoring Key
Ace = 15   King = 10   Queen = 5   Jack = 5   Number cards = the number shown
A *deck* is all 52 cards.   To *draw* means to take a card from the deck.

1. Draw five cards from the deck. Write the value of each card and the total score in the boxes below.

2. Add 6 to the score in *1*.

   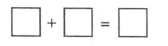

3. Draw three more cards and add their values together. Multiply the total score by 3. Add your answer to the score in *2*.

4. Draw two more cards. If you draw a King or a Queen, subtract 10 from the total score in *3*. If you draw an Ace, add 10. If you draw something else, do nothing.

   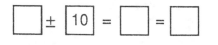

5. Draw four more cards and add their values to the total score in *4*.

6. The final total is: _____.

Continued

Purple Cows & Potato Chips ©1995 by Alta Book Center Publishers
Permission is granted to reproduce this page for classroom use.

Directions: *Work individually within a group (4 to 5 students).* You will need a pencil and a piece of paper. Follow the six steps below until everyone in the group gets the same answer. If you come up with different answers, try to find your mistakes. Then *share your answers with the class.*

Card Game B

Scoring Key

Ace = 15   King = 10   Queen = 5   Jack = 5   Number cards = the number shown
A *deck* is all 52 cards.   To *draw* means to take a card from the deck.

1. (First student) Draw two cards from the deck. Show them to the rest of the group.

2. (*Everyone* in the group) Write the value of each card and the total score in the boxes below. Do not show anyone in the group your total.

   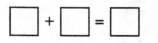

3. (*Next student*) Draw two more cards from the deck and show them to the other group members. Compute the total score.

   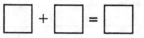

4. (*Everyone*) Add the total in *2.* to the total in *3.*

5. Repeat *3.* and *4.* until everyone in the group has had a turn.

6. (*Everyone*) Compare your answers.

2.3 Feeling Bags

Directions: *Work with a small group (3 to 5 students).* Your teacher will have several paper bags filled with objects. Pick one bag for your group. Reach inside it and touch an object. Describe what you're touching while each group member writes down what you say. Then ask each member to guess what the object is. After everyone guesses, reveal the object and pass the bag to another person in the group.

1. It feels . . . .

   hard

   smooth

   cold

   It's

   _____

2. It feels . . . .

   soft

   fuzzy

   round

   It's

   _____

3. It feels . . . .

   _____

   _____

   _____

   It's

   _____

4. It feels . . . .

   _____

   _____

   _____

   It's

   _____

5. It feels . . . .

   _____

   _____

   _____

   It's

   _____

6. It feels . . . .

   _____

   _____

   _____

   It's

   _____

2.4 Picture Stories

Directions: *Work with a small group (3 to 5 students).* Your teacher
will give you some magazines or catalogs. With your
group, select and cut out some pictures and glue them
onto colored paper. Write a story about the pictures and
five questions about the story. Then show the class the
pictures and ask the five questions. Write the answers
on the board. *Tell* the class your story (do not read it!)
and check the answers on the board when you finish
to see if they are correct.

Questions:

1. _____

   _____

   _____

2. _____

   _____

   _____

3. _____

   _____

   _____

4. _____

   _____

   _____

5. _____

   _____

   _____

2.5 Charades

Directions: *Work with a small group (3 to 5 students)*, but do your part *alone*. Choose a verb from the list below and try to act it out for your group. Your group will have one minute to guess what the verb is. (Don't repeat a verb that has already been used.) The group that guesses the most verbs in the time allowed wins.

Verbs:

argue	hiccough	read	study
bend	jog	run	swim
cough	jump	scratch	talk
drink	lie down	shrug	think
drive	laugh	sigh	wake up
eat	march	sit	walk
exercise	nudge	skip	wash
fly	pace	sleep	wink
get up	paint	stand up	write
giggle	pick up		

2.6 Body Language

Directions: *Work with a partner.* Your teacher will demonstrate the actions listed below. Try to guess the meaning of each action and a situation in which it might be used. Think of a sentence (question or statement) to go with the action. Are there other actions that you have seen and might not understand? *Ask your teacher and classmates about them.*

Action	Meaning	Sentence
1. Shaking head from left to right		
2. Nodding head up and down		
3. Moving extended index finger back and forth (or up and down).		
4. Shrugging the shoulders		
5. Rolling the eyes		
6. Looking up in the air and sighing		
7. Extending index finger (pointing upward)		
8. Waving the open hand back and forth, palm facing away		
9. Holding a hand up with the palm facing away		

Purple Cows & Potato Chips ©1995 by Alta Book Center Publishers
Permission is granted to reproduce this page for classroom use.

Continued

Action	Meaning	Sentence
10. Holding the arms akimbo, hands on waist		
11. Wrinkling the nose		
12. Making a circular motion with extended index finger pointed at head		
13. Tapping the toes		
14. Crossing the fingers		
15. Winking one eye and smiling		
16. Making a circle with thumb and index finger, other fingers extended		

2.7 Simon Says

Directions: *Work with a small group (5 to 7 students).* Your teacher will demonstrate this activity first. Then one member of your group will become "leader" and give commands. Remember, if a command begins with "Simon says," everyone should follow. If you follow the commands correctly, continue to play; if you do not, sit down. Continue to play until only one person in your group is standing. That person becomes the next "leader."

Here are some sample commands to get you started.

1. Shake your foot.
2. Scratch your nose.
3. Stick out your tongue.
4. Wiggle your fingers.
5. Turn around three times.
6. Take a giant step.
7. Take a baby step.
8. Touch your toes.
9. Touch your knees.
10. Walk backward.
11. Raise your left hand.
12. Look up.

Now write your own commands.

1. _____
2. _____
3. _____
4. _____
5. _____
6. _____
7. _____
8. _____
9. _____
10. _____

2.8 May I?

Directions: *Work with the rest of the class.* Your teacher will demonstrate this activity first. Then a student will be selected "leader." Remember, you may move only if you answer a question correctly and request permission by asking "May I?" If you ask permission, the answer will be, "Yes, you may." If you forget to ask before you move, or if you speak in your native language, you must return to the back of the room. The first person to reach the front of the room is the winner and the next "leader."

Write 12 questions you can ask when you become "leader."
Let your teacher check your work.

1. _____

2. _____

3. _____

4. _____

5. _____

6. _____

7. _____

8. _____

9. _____

10. _____

11. _____

12. _____

Purple Cows & Potato Chips ©1995 by Alta Book Center Publishers
Permission is granted to reproduce this page for classroom use.

2.9 Origami

Directions: *Work with a small group (3 to 5 students).* Your teacher will provide paper and scissors. Look at the origami patterns on this page and on pp. 48–53. Each member in your group should select a different pattern to follow. Read the instructions carefully and study the figures. Practice making the pattern you have chosen until you can successfully complete it. Then explain the procedure to the other group members. Do not look at the instructions or the figures. Demonstrate each step. You should learn from each group member how to make a different origami pattern. When you are done, *try writing down the instructions from memory.*

Fan

1. Take a square piece of paper and fold it in half (Figure 1).

FIGURE 1

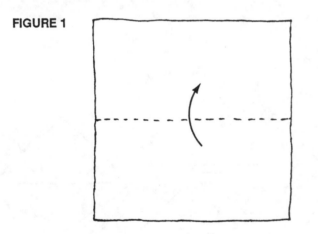

2. Continue folding the paper, forward then backwards, making narrow pleats (accordian style) along the long side of the paper (Figure 2).

FIGURE 2

3. Fold the pleated paper in half. Open up the pleated paper and paste or clip the two open sides together (Figure 3).

FIGURE 3

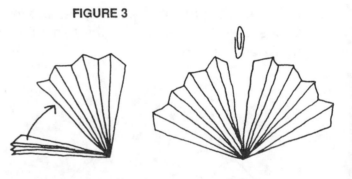

4. Tie a piece of string about one-half inch up from the bottom of your fan (Figure 4).

FIGURE 4

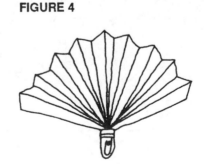

Continued

Teacup

1. Take a square piece of paper and fold it in half to make a triangle (Figure 1).

FIGURE 1

2. Fold the left corner of the triangle to the middle of the opposite side (Figure 2). Do the same thing with the right corner (Figure 3).

FIGURE 2　　　　　　　　**FIGURE 3**

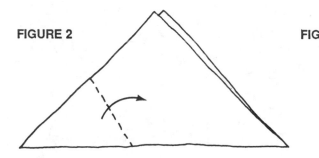

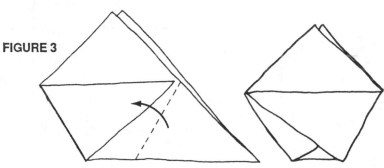

3. Fold down the front flap (Figure 4). Do the same thing with the back flap (Figure 5).

FIGURE 4　　　　　　**FIGURE 5**

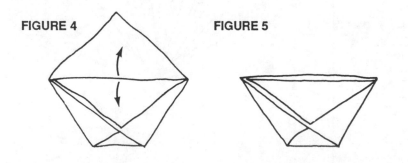

Purple Cows & Potato Chips ©1995 by Alta Book Center Publishers
Permission is granted to reproduce this page for classroom use.

Airplane

1. Take a rectangular piece of paper and fold it in half lengthwise. Make a sharp crease with your thumb. (Figure 1).

FIGURE 1

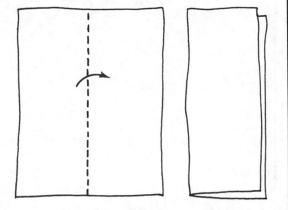

2. Fold one corner of the paper back along the crease (Figure 2).

FIGURE 2

Turn the paper over and repeat Step 2 (Figure 3).

FIGURE 3

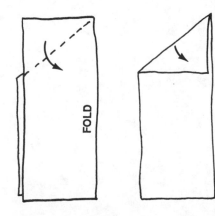

3. Take the folded side and fold it inward once again, halfway toward the crease (Figure 4).

FIGURE 4

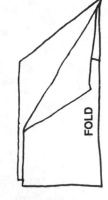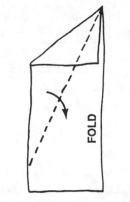

4. Turn the paper over and repeat Step 3 (Figure 5).

FIGURE 5

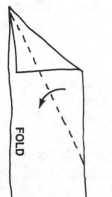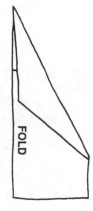

5. Turn the paper in a horizontal position and fold the top part down (Figure 6).

FIGURE 6

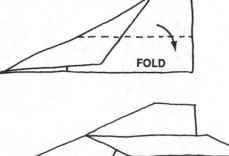

(Airplane)

6. Turn the paper over and repeat Step 5 (Figure 7).

    FIGURE 7

    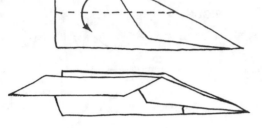

7. Hold the folded paper in a horizontal position and open up the wings of the airplane (Figure 8).

    FIGURE 8

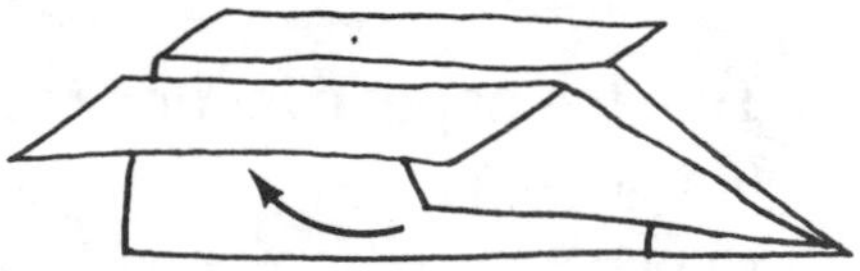

    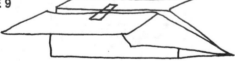

8. Tape together the wings of the airplane at the center and tilt them upwards slightly (Figure 9).

    FIGURE 9

Purple Cows & Potato Chips ©1995 by Alta Book Center Publishers
Permission is granted to reproduce this page for classroom use.

Windmill

1. Take a square piece of paper and fold each side halfway toward the center (Figure 1).

FIGURE 1

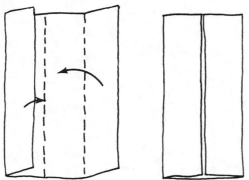

2. Turn the paper over and fold it in half (Figure 2).

FIGURE 2

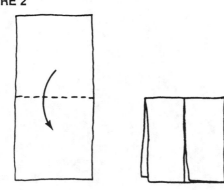

3. Fold the front side of the paper in half to the top fold (Figure 3).

FIGURE 3

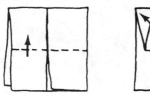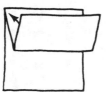

4. Pull out the inside corner on each side (Figure 4).

FIGURE 4

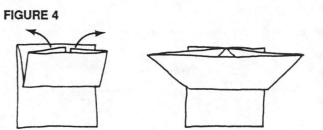

5. Turn the paper over and repeat Steps 3 and 4 (Figure 5).

FIGURE 5

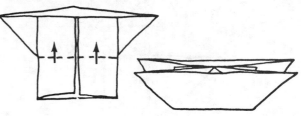

6. Fold the right corner of the folded paper toward the center (Figure 6).

FIGURE 6

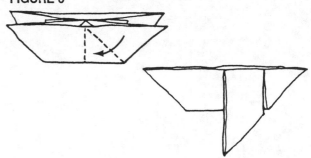

7. Turn the paper over and repeat Step 6
   (Figure 7).

FIGURE 7

8. Flatten out the paper and open up the
   windmill (Figure 8).

FIGURE 8

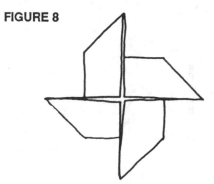

Bug Catcher

1. Take a square piece of paper and fold it in half to make a triangle (Figure 1).

   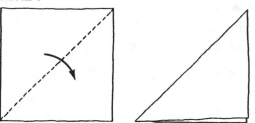

2. Fold the triangle in half; then open up the paper and flatten it out (Figure 2).

   FIGURE 2

   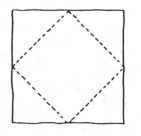

   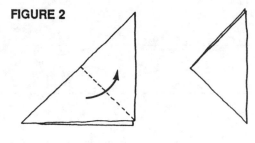

3. Turn the paper over and fold all four corners toward the center to make a square (Figure 3).

   FIGURE 3

   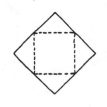

4. Fold the square in half and in half again (Figure 4).

   FIGURE 4

5. Open up the square again, place your thumbs and index fingers under the flaps and push the paper toward the center (Figure 5).

   FIGURE 5

   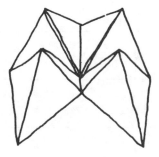

2.10 Money Game

Directions: *Work with a partner.* Your teacher will bring catalogs and newspaper advertisements to class. With your partner, imagine that you have $250 to spend together. Decide what items you will buy. They should be things you need and want right now. You must agree with your partner on the items. Write the items and their cost on the chart below. (Remember: Don't go over $250.)
Share your list with the rest of the class.

Item	Cost
1.	
2.	
3.	
4.	
5.	
6.	
7.	
8.	
9.	
10.	
11.	
12.	

Purple Cows & Potato Chips ©1995 by Alta Book Center Publishers Permission is granted to reproduce this page for classroom use.

2.11 Aerobics

Directions: *Work with a partner.* Take turns following and giving the directions below. Then take turns giving the same directions to your partner and another pair of students. Make sure that all three students are standing so that they cannot see one another. See if everyone follows the directions in exactly the same way.

1. **Arm Lift (front and side)**
   Place your arms at your sides.
   Raise your arms shoulder high.
   Return them to your sides.

   Raise your arms overhead until your hands touch.
   Return your arms to your sides.
   Raise your arms overhead, clap your hands.
   Return your arms to your sides.
   Repeat.

   Raise your arms shoulder high.
   Swing them forward until your hands touch.
   Swing your arms back.
   Swing your arms forward and clap your hands.
   Swing your arms back.
   Lower your arms to your sides.

2. **Leg Lift**
   Stand with your feet together, arms at your sides.
   Bend your left knee and raise your foot a few inches off the floor.
   Lower your foot to the floor.
   Repeat four times, gradually lifting your foot to waist height.
   Stamp your left foot on the floor.
   Repeat everything using your right foot.

3. **Waist Bend**
   Bend from the waist, twice to the left.
   Bend from the waist, twice to the right.
   Bend forward and back twice each.
   Turn all the way around, once to the left and once to the right.

4. **Step Slide**
   Step slide to the left.
   Step slide to the right.
   Do two short knee bends.
   Turn all the way around.
   Step slide forward and step slide back.
   Do two short knee bends.
   Turn all the way around.
   Repeat everything.

5. **Head Bounce**
   Bounce your head forward four times.
   Bounce your head right four times.
   Bounce your head back four times.
   Bounce your head forward, right, back, and left twice, slowly.
   Reverse the direction and repeat everything.

2.12 Sentence Starters

Directions: *Work with the rest of the class.* Introduce yourself to a classmate. Then ask that classmate to complete one of the statements below. Write down the person's response and name next to the statement. Ask a different classmate to respond to another statement. Continue interviewing other students until your exercise sheet is complete. *Be sure to write down each student's name and share your responses with the rest of the class.*

1. My favorite food is_____

2. I like this class because_____

3. My teacher is_____

4. If I had $500, I would_____

5. College is _____

6. The color I like best is_____ because _____

7. Television is _____

8. My favorite thing to do on weekends is_____

9. The most difficult thing about English is_____

10. People who ride bicycles are _____

11. Studying is _____

12. In five years I want to be _____

_____

Purple Cows & Potato Chips ©1995 by Alta Book Center Publishers
Permission is granted to reproduce this page for classroom use.

2.13 Perfect Match

Directions: *Work alone.* Complete each of the statements below by circling **a**, **b**, or **c**. Then listen carefully as your teacher explains what to do next.

1. A perfect Saturday night is

   a. a symphony concert and dessert

   b. a fancy, expensive dinner and a walk in the moonlight

   c. a large combination pizza and a good James Bond movie

2. A perfect movie is

   a. a romantic comedy with lots of rock and roll music

   b. a wild, jungle rescue adventure

   c. a mystery with helicopters, computer wizards, fast cars, guns, and
      beautiful women

3. A perfect day off is

   a. a long drive in the country

   b. shopping in the big city

   c. cleaning and fixing little things around the house;
      putting my home in order

4. A perfect vacation is

   a. swimming, sunning, sailing, dancing on a sunny island

   b. sight-seeing, shopping, eating at good restaurants in a faraway city

   c. relaxing at home with my family

5. A perfect pet is

   a. a big, old, loving, friendly, playful dog

   b. a quiet, beautiful, independent cat

   c. a large goldfish in an outdoor pond

6. Perfect clothes are

   a. comfortable, inexpensive, "wash and wear"

   b. elegant, well-made, expensive

   c. fashionable, fun to wear, bright colors

2.14 Preference Grids

Directions: *Work alone.* Look at the grid below and the boxes numbered 1. to 9. Each number represents a preference: 1. = like/agree with the most; 9. = dislike/disagree with the most. Now read the directions for exercise sheet, p. 59.

Continued

Directions: *Work alone.* Listen as your teacher asks different students about the things they like to do. If you like or agree with a student's answer, write it down in one of the squares below. When all of your squares are filled, cut or tear them out and place them on your grid in order of your preference (1.–9.). *Share your completed grid with the class.*

THUNDERSTORMS

Notes to the Teacher

3.1 Sound Effects

For this activity you will need to tape record a series of 12 common sounds. The sounds take a little time to record, but they can be used over and over for this activity as well as for activity 3.3 Sound Bingo. We suggest sounds such as these: silverware rattling in a drawer; a tea kettle whistling; a toilet flushing; a spoon stirring in a cup; an alarm clock going off; a door closing; a dishwasher running; a telephone ringing; water running; a doorbell ringing; an egg timer buzzing; a vacuum cleaner running; someone typing.

As you play the tape, allow students enough time to discuss each sound and to describe it on their exercise sheets (*one* sheet per pair). The large group sharing at the end of class is the important part of this activity. Avoid giving the correct answers until all students have had a chance to share their responses.

3.2 Music Composition

For this activity, tape record five different musical selections. Don't record the entire selection; one minute or less for each selection is sufficient. Once you have the selections taped, you can use them repeatedly. The selections (for instruments only, no singing) should be varied–classical, jazz, blues, country- and should each elicit different feeling and images.

Allow students time to record their impressions on the exercise sheet (*one* sheet per pair). Here again, the follow-up group sharing and discussion are most important. A fun extension activity is to have students listen to the selections a second time and suggest titles for each one.

3.3 Sound Bingo

For this activity, use the 12 sounds you recorded for activity 3.1. First, make an Exercise Key like the Sample below, filling in the names of the 12 sounds under each letter. Next, make five copies of the blank student SOUND card (p. 69) and number them from 1 to 5. Then, randomly fill in the boxes under each letter with the names of five sounds. Finally, make multiple copies of the five SOUND cards. Now you are ready to do the activity.

Exercise Key

Card # _____

S	O	U	N	D
Tea kettle	Water running	Typewriter	Toilet flushing	Alarm clock
Silverware	Alarm clock	Doorbell	Water running	Dishwasher
Toilet flushing	Dishwasher	Toilet flushing	Tea kettle	Door closing
Vacuum	Doorbell	Eggtimer	Door closing	Vacuum
Telephone	Eggtimer	Water running	Vacuum	Telephone

Working in groups of five is preferable. Each student in the group picks a SOUND card with a different number. (If you want to be able to use the cards again, have students mark in pencil.) Begin the activity by saying one of the letters, for example, "S." Then play a sound. Students look on their cards under "S" for the name of that sound. If they find the name, they mark it with an X. You mark the sound under "S" on the Exercise Key. Continue playing sounds and marking boxes until one or more students have completed a row with X's. Check and discuss answers. It is always fun to award prizes to the winners.

3.4 Paralanguage

For this activity, each group needs one exercise sheet, and should appoint a secretary. Before presenting the activity, practice making the sounds so you can repeat them easily and without confusion. Allow students ample time to discuss and write down possible meanings and appropriate expressions for each sound.

3.5 Sounds Like a _____

Before presenting this activity, work through the sounds, making certain you have a one-word or several-word association for each sound. Having students repeat different sounds themselves is humorous and can lead to an informative discussion of similar sounds and their meanings in other cultures.

3.6 What's That Noise?

Students may be able to contribute to this activity, offering objects and sounds from their native countries and languages.

3.7 What's in Your Pocket?

The day before you do this activity, tell students to bring an object to class to describe. The object should be small enough to fit in a pocket or purse. Give students ten to 12 minutes to work on the exercise sheets alone before you break the class into groups.

3.8 Sing a Song

This activity requires advance planning, as students need to prepare their songs and bring in musical equipment. Distribute the exercise sheet a few days ahead so that students can make copies of the song lyrics for their classmates. You will also need to bring in a cassette and/or record player.

We have found that a teacher-led song helps break the ice and is a necessary ingredient for sharing later on. A simple repetitive song works best. For example, if you play the guitar at all, you can play "Skip to My Lou" because it has only two basic chords. Students enjoy adding extra verses.

SKIP TO MY LOU

D
Skip, skip, skip to my Lou,

A7
Skip, skip, skip to my Lou,

D
Skip, skip, skip to my Lou,

A7   **D**
Skip to my Lou my darling.

Lost my partner, what'll I do?
Lost my partner, what'll I do?
Lost my partner, what'll I do?
Skip to my Lou my darling.

I'll get another one prettier'n you....
Flies in the buttermilk, shoo, fly, shoo....
Little red wagon painted blue....

As students add verses, repeat the chorus, "Skip, skip" after each one.

3.9 Listening Fantasy

Instruct your students to just relax and listen. They should not take notes; they will not be tested. Ask students to shut their eyes while you read the following fantasy. You can add details if you wish.

"Let's imagine we are going on a picnic to the mountains. We will leave tomorrow morning. We will take a lunch, of course, and plan to spend the afternoon hiking, taking pictures, watching the birds and wildlife, and enjoying the fresh mountain air.

I have the perfect place in mind. We will have to drive about three hours to get there. The picnic spot is in the mountains near a small stream and a lake. The mountain road is bumpy sometimes and a little dusty, but at last we arrive at the exact spot I have in mind.

There is one other family already here, and the parents are preparing the picnic lunch under a big tree. There is a large blanket, a picnic basket, and a big bottle on a table.

Keep this picture clearly in your mind. Try to remember what everything looks like. Do you have it in your mind? Now you can open your eyes."

Allow students to work in small groups sharing their answers to the questions on the exercise sheet. Follow up with a large group sharing and discussion.

3.10 Sounds Inventory

For this activity, you will need to copy the exercise sheet and distribute it to students the day before. Explain that students are to write down 20 sounds they hear during the day. The next day follow up with a small group sharing and then a large group sharing. Ask questions such as "Did anyone hear the same sound?... What was the most unusual sound?... What sound was heard most often?... Where were you when you heard that sound?... Who or what made that sound?" and so on.

3.11 Listening Chain

To do this activity, students must understand the concept of word association. Before beginning the activity, do a large group word association using familiar words such as *school, Friday, lunch,* and so on. Make sure students understand the associations and share their lists at the end of class. (Students can add more words to the list given.)

3.12 Listening Clues

Have students work with partners and read them the following listening clues. Allow time for students to discuss and record their guesses. There can be more than one correct answer. See how many ideas students can generate for each listening clue.

1. It will not roll off a desk or table. It can be opened or closed, but not locked. (*Answer:* a book.)
2. It is easy to catch. It is hard to get rid of. (*Answer:* a cold.)
3. They are very cheap to buy. Campers and smokers find them useful. (*Answer:* matches.)
4. It is easy to find. It is cheaper to use on Saturdays. (*Answer:* a telephone.)
5. It can be recycled. It is a good insulator. (*Answer:* a newspaper.)
6. It requires no gasoline. You don't have to feed it. (*Answer:* a bicycle.)
7. They are good for people who want to be anonymous. They are difficult to see with in the dark. (*Answer:* sunglasses.)
8. They provide protection. Sometimes they are flat. (*Answer:* shoes.)
9. It is high in calories. You can buy it plain or crunchy. (*Answer:* peanut butter.)
10. It comes in many colors. It is worn on the body. (*Answer:* nail polish.)

A good follow-up is to have students generate their own clues and answers. Have them work in small groups and then share the clues with the entire class.

3.13 The Art of Listening

Give each student in a pair *one* exercise sheet (p. 79 *or* p. 80). Review the directions and allow ten to 12 minutes for students to complete their drawings, and additional time for picture comparisons. Then distribute the second exercise sheet and repeat the activity with the second partner doing the drawing.

3.14 Interviews

This activity consists of three interviews that may be done over a period of days. In the first and third interviews, students interview each other, while in the second interview they question an American outside of class. Prior to beginning Interview #2, you may wish to lead a class discussion focusing on appropriate interview behavior: how to approach, engage, and thank an interview subject. You will need double copies of the exercise sheet for Interview #3 and single copies of the exercise sheets for Interviews #1 and #2.

A good way to follow up each interview is to hold a whole-class question-answer session using the information students have obtained. Here are some sample questions:

Interview #1
1. How many people have some family members here with them? How many are here alone? What special things can we do to help people from being lonely? What can we do to feel better when we miss our family and home?
2. What is good about having friends? What kinds of good things do friends provide for us? What is one special thing about your friend? Do you have a special friend here in _____ ?
3. What kinds of things make for a good day? What do we do that brings us happiness or peaceful feelings?
4. What kinds of things make us angry? Do some of us get angry about the same things? Who has a bad temper? Who hardly ever gets angry? What do you do when you get angry? Do you break things? Yell? Sulk? Cry?
5. What can we cook? How about a pot-luck!
6. What sorts of things do we count as successes? What areas of our lives are measured in terms of "success?" Work? School? Sports?
7. When you buy clothes, how do you decide what to buy? Cheap? Expensive? Classic? Modern style? Comfortable? Washable?
8. What kinds of cars do we like? Why? What kinds of cars do we have now? Why?
9. What are good ages for marriage? Why?
10. What is a good sized family? Why? Who comes from a large family? Who comes from a small one? What things does each size family have to offer?

Interview #2
1. How many Americans liked to travel? Where did they like to travel? Do they speak foreign languages? Which ones?
2. Where do Americans like to travel in the United States?
3. What kinds of five-year plans do Americans have?
4. Were your interviewees happy with their work? What other kinds of work would they rather be doing?
5. What kinds of things make American people happy?
6. What were the problems people felt were important in the U.S.A.?
7. What T.V. shows or movies were named as popular? Any movie stars?

Interview #3
1. Which student in your class got up first in the morning?
2. Who studied the longest yesterday?
3. How long did he or she study?
4. Who did the same things at the same time?
5. Who ate dinner the latest?
6. Who went to class first?
7. Who did the most unusual thing?
8. What things did your classmates do in their free time?

3.1 Sound Effects

Directions: *Work with a partner.* Listen to the sounds your teacher plays. With your partner, identify each sound and write what it is on the chart below. After you have identified all 12 sounds, *discuss your answers with the class.* Check your answers with your teacher. Did you recognize all the sounds?

Sound	What is it?
1.	
2.	
3.	
4.	
5.	
6.	
7.	
8.	
9.	
10.	
11.	
12.	

3.2 Music Notes

Directions: *Work with a small group (3 to 5 students).* Your teacher will play five short musical selections. Relax and listen to the music. After each selection is over, answer the questions about it on the chart below. When you have listened to all the selections and answered the questions, *share your answers with the class.*

Musical Selection	What are you thinking of?	How do you feel?
1.		
2.		
3.		
4.		
5.		

3.3 Sound Bingo

Directions: *Work with a small group (4 to 5 students).* Your teacher will give you a card labeled SOUND. Then he or she will play a tape of 12 different sounds. Before playing each sound, your teacher will tell you to look under a letter on your SOUND card (for example, the letter "S"). Listen to the sound and see if its name is listed on your card under that letter. If it is, mark that box with an **X**. The person who fills all the boxes in a row up and down, across, or diagonally, is the winner. *Check your answers with the teacher and the class.*

Card # _____

S	O	U	N	D

3.4 Paralanguage

Directions: *Work with a small group (4 to 5 students).* Look at the sounds listed in the chart below. As your teacher demonstrates each sound, discuss its meaning(s) with your group. Think of a sentence that might go with the sound and have the group "secretary" write it down. (For example, *sound* "Whew!" *meaning* "What a relief!" or "Thank goodness!" *sentence* "I arrived just in time!") *Share your answers with the class.*

	Sound	Meaning	Sentence
1.	Ooooooops. . .	a small accident	Oops, you broke your cup!
2.	Uh-oh		
3.	Ah hah!!!		
4.	Mmmmmmmm,		
5.	Tsk! Tsk!		
6.	Ouch!		
7.	Shhh . . .		
8.	Uh-huh.		
9.	Humphf!		
10.	Hah!		
11.	Huh-uh.		
12.	Hmmm.		

3.5 Sounds Like a _____

Directions: *Work with a partner.* Look at the list of sounds below. Try to think of an animal or object that makes each sound. Write your answer next to the sound described. *Share your answers with the class.*

Sound	What makes the sound?
1. Clip-clop-clip-clop	
2. Caw-caw-caw-caw	
3. Gobble-gobble-gobble	
4. Eek! Eek! Eek!	
5. Baa-a Baa-a	
6. Chirp chirp chirp	
7. Mooo-o Mooo-o	
8. Meow meow meow	
9. Quack quack quack	
10. Buzzzzz buzzzzz	
11. Oink oink oink	
12. Whoo-o-o-ooo who-o-o-ooo	
13. Coo-coo	
14. Woof-woof	
15. Hee-haw	

3.6 What's That Noise?

Directions: *Work with a partner.* Read each word listed under "Object" and match it with a corresponding word or phrase under "Sound". *Share your answers with the class.*

Object	Sound
1. Birds	a. Buzz buzz
2. A heavy object hitting the ground	b. Rattle rattle
3. A bee	c. Plop
4. A guitar string	d. Warble warble
5. An old car	e. Thud
6. Soda pop in a glass	f. Jingle
7. Breaking a pencil	g. Ding-dong
8. Keys on a ring	h. Snap
9. A snake	i. Hiss
10. A doorbell	j. Twang
11. Dropping something into water	k. Fizz

3.7 What's in Your Pocket?

Directions: *Work alone first, then work with a small group (4 to 5 students).* Think of something you have with you in your pocket or purse. Describe that object by writing answers to the following questions. Then, in a group, take turns describing your object and having everyone guess what it is. If nobody guesses the object after two minutes, show the group what it is.

1. What shape is it? __ _____

_____

_____

2. What color is it? _____

_____

_____

3. What is it made of? _____

_____

_____

4. How does it feel? _____

_____

_____

5. What is it used for? _____

_____

_____

6. How does it work? _____

_____

_____

3.8 Sing a Song

Directions: *Work with a partner or small group (3 to 5 students).*
Think of a song that you would like the class to hear
or learn. Bring in a musical instrument to play while you
sing the song yourself (or with another student), or bring
in a tape or record to play. Have the class guess what
the song is about before you tell them its meaning and
what you like about the music. The song can be in your
native language or in English.

Write the words to your song here:

_____

_____

_____

_____

_____

_____

_____

_____

3.9 Listening Fantasy

Directions: *Work alone and then with a small group (3 to 4 students).* Listen as your teacher describes a fantasy experience. Let your mind flow easily and imagine that you are in the situation being described. Then, with your group, discuss answers to the questions below. Listen carefully to each other. There will be many different answers depending on your imagination and the details you add.

1. How many children are there? _____

2. What do the children look like? _____

3. How are they dressed? _____

4. What colors are their clothes? _____

5. What are they playing? _____

6. What is in the picnic basket? _____

7. What is in the bottle? _____

8. How far away are the trees? _____

9. What kind of trees are they? _____

10. What does the blanket look like? _____

11. How does the blanket feel? _____

12. How big is the blanket? _____

3.10 Sounds Inventory

Directions: *Work alone.* Make an inventory of 20 different sounds you hear during the day. Write those sounds on the list below. Bring your list to class and *share the names of the sounds with your classmates.*

Sounds

1. _____
2. _____
3. _____
4. _____
5. _____
6. _____
7. _____
8. _____
9. _____
10. _____
11. _____
12. _____
13. _____
14. _____
15. _____
16. _____
17. _____
18. _____
19. _____
20. _____

3.11 Listening Chain

Directions: *Work with a small group (3 to 5 students).* Choose a word from the list below and say it to your group. Ask each group member to contribute another word associated with the first word (for example, *Keys*: lock; door; car; lost). Do that until no more associations can be made. Appoint one group member to write down all the word associations. Allow no more than *15 seconds* to pass between words. If you don't understand an association, ask the group member to explain it. *Share your word association lists with the class.* See which group has the most words.

Words

1. Keys _____

2. Metal _____

3. Suitcase _____

4. Ink _____

5. Letters _____

6. Dress _____

7. Dirt _____

8. Paper _____

9. Square _____

10. Garden _____

11. Knife _____

12. Napkin _____

3.12 Listening Clues

Directions: *Work with a partner.* Listen carefully as your teacher gives you ten listening clues. Discuss each clue with your partner and then write on the list below what you think it describes.

What you think the clue describes:

1. _____

2. _____

3. _____

4. _____

5. _____

6. _____

7. _____

8. _____

9. _____

10. _____

3.13 The Art of Listening

Directions: *Work with a partner.* Do not show your partner your exercise sheet! When your teacher tells you to begin, try to explain to your partner how to draw the picture below. When your teacher tells you to stop, show the picture to your partner and compare it with his or her drawing. *Share the drawing with the class.*

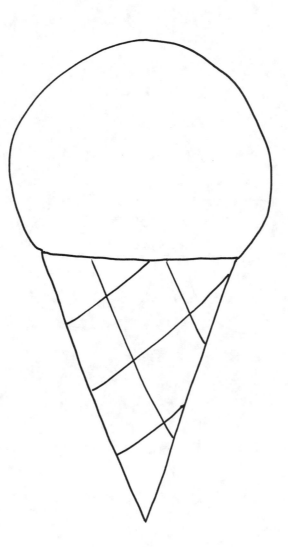

Continued

Directions: *Work with a partner.* Do not show your partner your exercise sheet! When your teacher tells you to begin, try to explain to your partner how to draw the picture below. When your teacher tells you to stop, show the picture to your partner and compare it with his or her drawing. *Share the drawing with the class.*

Directions: *Work with a partner.* Take turns interviewing one another. Write your partner's responses on this sheet. When your interviews are finished, *share your information with the class.*

Name _____

Native Country _____

1. Do you have family in this city or country? _____

2. Who is a very important friend for you? _____

3. What was the best part of your day yesterday? _____

4. What kinds of things make you angry sometimes? _____

5. What are two things you like to cook and eat? _____

6. What is one big success you have had in your life? _____

7. Do you dress differently now than you did two years ago? How? Why? _____

8. What kind of car would you like to buy if you had a lot of money? _____

9. What is a good age for women to get married? For men? _____

10. What is a good size family to have? _____

Continued

Directions: *Work alone.* Using this exercise sheet, interview an American outside of class. You may interview anyone of any age or occupation. Bring the completed exercise sheet to class and *share the information you have collected.*

Introduction

Hello. My name is _____ . I am from _____ .

I would be grateful if you could help me. I am in an English class and my teacher wants me to interview an American. I would like to find out what you think about some subjects. I have nine (9) questions to ask you. It will only take a few minutes. I appreciate your help.

Questions

1. Do you like to travel? _____

2. What countries have you visited? _____
   _____

3. Do you speak any foreign languages? _____ Which one(s)? _____
   _____

4. Where have you traveled in the United States? _____
   _____

5. What would you like to be doing five years from now? _____
   _____

6. Do you like your work now? Is there any work you would rather do? _____
   _____

7. What are three things that make you happy? _____
   _____

8. What do you think the most important problem is in the U.S.A. today? _____
   _____

9. What kind of movies or T.V. shows do you like best? _____
   _____

Continued

Directions: *Work alone, then with a partner.* Your teacher will give you two copies of this exercise sheet. On one copy, write down your daily schedule below. Then share your schedule with your partner and write down his or her schedule on the second copy. When you have both finished, *share your information with the class.*

Time of the Day	Activity

Unit 4

POTATO CHIPS

Unit 4
Notes to the Teacher

4.1 Herbs and Verbs

For this activity you will need to bring eight jars of herbs to class. Number the jars using masking tape, self-sticking labels, or foil. Good herbs to bring in are rosemary, dill weed, bay leaves, sweet basil, anise, marjoram, garlic, sage, thyme, fennel, ginger root, cilantro, parsley, licorice root, camomile. Students may have trouble translating the names of certain herbs as they know them from their native languages into English.

4.2 Native Cuisine

Since this activity requires advance preparation, announce it two or three days ahead in class. Discuss the foods people bring to "potluck" parties in the United States. Get tentative ideas from your students about what foods they might want to bring. (You may want to have a sign-up sheet for main dishes, desserts, salads, breads, etc., to avoid having 11 bags of potato chips!)

4.3 Peanut Butter and Bananas

For this activity, you will need to bring to class the following items:

4 bananas	paper plates
1 small jar of peanut butter	paper napkins
1 table knife	

During this activity you will prepare two sandwiches, which you will cut into four pieces each, to share with the class. If you have a large class, make three or four sandwiches ahead of time so you will have enough to go around when it is time to share. (Not everyone will want to taste your peanut butter and banana delicacy!) Allow time for clean up and to check students' written directions.

4.4 Soft and Chewy or Hard and Crunchy?

For this activity you will need to bring to class foods that are soft, chewy, hard, or crunchy. We suggest the following foods: small lemon slices, small dill pickle slices, and small bits of chocolate. Be sure to bring enough to go around the class. Also bring peanuts, pretzels, miniature marshmallows, cheese cubes, sliced celery, or any other bite-sized taste treat.

Arrange the foods on paper plates in front of the class and entice students to sample each item. Allow time for clean up and taste comparisons.

4.5 What Parts of a Plant Do We Eat?

To supplement this activity, you might want to bring in examples of root, stem, leaf, fruit, seed, and flower foods. Also bring food pictures that illustrate the six categories. Answers for the exercise sheet are:

Roots:	carrots, radishes, yellow onions, beets, sweet potatoes, potatoes
Stems:	celery, broccoli, asparagus, rhubarb, swiss chard
Leaves:	celery, spinach, lettuce, cabbage, swiss chard, beets, mustard greens
Fruit:	apples, pears, bananas, oranges, peaches, zucchini, strawberries
Seeds:	sunflower seeds, rice, beans, corn, peas, lentils
Flowers:	broccoli, cauliflower, artichokes, zucchini

4.6 Spice Hunt

For this activity you will need to bring in a variety of spices (at least twelve different ones). Put about 1 teaspoon of each spice into separate small paper cups, and number the cups. Allow students to look at and smell the spices. Suggested spices appear on the exercise sheet, or you can add your own.

4.7 The Nose Knows

For this activity, fill ten jars with the following items: lemon slices, peppermint extract, vanilla extract, rubbing alcohol, perfume, cinnamon, ammonia, strong-smelling cheese, and two other items of your choice. Completely cover the containers with foil, and make a hole in the top of the foil with a pencil. Number each container. Make a master answer key before you distribute the exercise sheet to your students.

4.8 Pudding Me On!

Bring the following items to class:

1 package each of pudding vanilla, chocolate, banana, and butterscotch	measuring cups 4 large spoons paper towels
2 quarts of milk paper cups	plastic spoons

Arrange those items on a table in front of the class. Divide students into four groups, if possible. (If you have more than 20 students, you will need more materials or you will have to skip the activity this time.) Allow time for clean up and friendly conversation.

4.9 Salad Daze

This is a two-day activity, one day to plan the salad and one day to prepare and eat it. On the first day, discuss with students what ingredients a good vegetable salad and good dressing require. Get volunteers to bring in specific ingredients. You bring the bowls, knives, cutting boards, paper plates, and plastic forks, or have students volunteer to bring them. On the second day, make sure students understand beforehand what they are responsible for in preparing the salad with their group.

4.10 Safety First!

Many of our students have trouble reading labels and often confuse food items, cleaning items, and personal hygiene items. Often, too, students need help reading the labels for information about the correct use and storage of the items. This activity should help students become more informed consumers.

Bring in ten of the following items or similar ones from your home cupboards (any brand will do). Number each item.

household ammonia	cough syrup
mouthwash	hand lotion
chlorine bleach	rubber cement
rubbing alcohol	turpentine or
soy sauce	paint thinner
hair conditioner	liquid laundry
nail-polish remover	detergent
antacid liquid	aspirin
vinegar	furniture polish

Arrange the items on a table in front of the class. Emphasize that students must not taste these things, only look, read, and smell (with care!). Allow time for a large group sharing.

4.11 Name the Perfume

The day before doing this activity, ask your students to bring in some perfumes or fragrances for men and women. Or, plan to bring in ten numbered bottles of fragrances yourself. Cover the names on the bottles. Allow enough time for a group sharing of the answers.

4.12 Taste Test

You or your students should bring to class two cans of each of the following colas: Classic Coke, New Coke, Cherry Coke, Dr. Pepper, and Pepsi (ten cans in all). Cover the cans with foil and number them (you will have several cans numbered 1, several numbered 2, 3, etc.). Give students a specific period of time to taste a little bit of each cola and to write their guesses on their exercise sheets. Have students compare answers at the end of class.

4.13 Popcorn Popping

For this activity, you will need to reserve the school's kitchen or bring to class an electric frying pan (and an extension cord, if needed). You will also need to provide all of the ingredients for making popcorn and a container to put the popped corn in. The usual ingredients are: 1 bag or can of unpopped popcorn; oil; salt (optional); margarine or butter (optional); a butter knife, bowl(s), and potholders.

When students have completed their lists of instructions, have them dictate a final procedure for you to write on the board. Then ask a student to make popcorn according to the dictated procedure. If all goes well, you will end up with fresh popcorn for the entire class.

4.14 Lemon Aid

For this activity you will need a half dozen or so lemons, depending on the size of your class, paper plates, and a utility knife. Quarter the lemons and place them on the paper plates, one plate per group. If time and interest allow, you can follow up with preparation of a lemon treat the next day, in or out of class.

4.1 Herbs and Verbs

Directions: *Work with a small group (3 to 4 students).* Your teacher will have eight numbered containers of herbs. Bring two containers at a time to your table and work with your group to answer the questions below. Write the common English name for the herb if you know it, or check your dictionary if you know the name in your native language but not in English. *Compare your answers with those of the rest of the class.*

Jar	How does the herb smell?	How is it used?	Herb
1.	sour, sharp	for making pickles and to put in yogurt salad	dill weed
2.			
3.			
4.			
5.			
6.			
7.			
8.			

Purple Cows & Potato Chips ©1995 by Alta Book Center Publishers
Permission is granted to reproduce this page for classroom use.

4.2 Native Cuisine

Directions: *Work with a classmate or alone.* Your teacher will ask you to bring a special food to class to share with everyone. You can bring any food you want, from your own country or another, but it should be something simple and easy to prepare. After you have tasted all the foods, write answers to the questions below. *Share your answers with the class.*

1. Which of the foods do you like best? _____

2. Who brought that food? _____

3. Describe that food. How does it taste? What are the ingredients? (If you don't know, make a guess.) _____

   _____

4. Which foods are new to you? _____

   _____

5. Which foods are desserts? _____

   _____

6. Which foods are snack foods? _____

   _____

7. Which ones are salty? _____

8. Which foods are hard and crunchy? _____

   _____

9. Which foods are soft and sweet? _____

   _____

10. Which food is most unusual? Try to describe what is in it. _____

   _____

11. Which food would you like to try again? _____

12. Which food would you like the recipe for? _____

4.3 Peanut Butter and Bananas

Directions: *Work with a partner.* Your teacher will demonstrate
how to make a peanut butter and banana sandwich.
With your partner, first write down all the ingredients
your teacher brings to class.

   Then, as the teacher is making the sandwich, one
partner watches and describes the demonstration (for
example: "The teacher is picking up the loaf of bread . . .
Now she or he is opening the bag . . .") while the other
partner looks away. The partner who is describing should
make sure the other partner understands every step.

   When the demonstration is over, all the partners
who did not watch will face the teacher and explain how
to make the same sandwich. The teacher will follow the
instructions carefully and share all the sandwiches with
you. While you are eating your sandwich, with your
partner write down all the directions for making a
peanut butter and banana sandwich.

Ingredients (What we need)

1. _____   4. _____

2. _____   5. _____

3. _____   6. _____

Directions (What we do)

1. _____

2. _____

3. _____

4. _____

5. _____

6. _____

7. _____

8. _____

9. _____

10. _____

Purple Cows & Potato Chips ©1995 by Alta Book Center Publishers
Permission is granted to reproduce this page for classroom use.

4.4 Soft and Chewy or Hard and Crunchy

Directions: *Work alone.* Your teacher will bring six different foods to class. Taste each food, then look at the chart below. Try to identify the taste of each food by marking the boxes under the words that describe it. *Share your answers with the class.*

Food	Hard	Crunchy	Salty	Soft	Chewy	Sweet	Sour	Juicy	Bitter	Delicious	Creamy	Sticky	Dry	Moist	Mushy	Terrible
1.																
2.																
3.																
4.																
5.																
6.																

4.5 What Parts of a Plant Do We Eat?

Directions: *Work with a partner.* We eat many different parts of plants. Read the list of foods below. Then read the list with your partner, decide what part of a plant each food is. Write the name of that food under the correct plant part. (Some foods can be in more than one category; for example, broccoli is a stem *and* a flower.) Discuss how you have seen the different foods prepared. *Share your answers with the class.*

Foods

Carrots	Broccoli	Asparagus	Rhubarb	Cabbage
Apples	Zucchini	Lettuce	Artichokes	Strawberries
Celery	Pears	Rice	Corn	Beets
Cauliflower	Bananas	Oranges	Lentils	Potatoes
Spinach	Sunflower Seeds	Sweet Potatoes	Peas	Swiss Chard
Radishes	Yellow Onions	Beans	Peaches	Mustard Greens

Roots

1. _____
2. _____
3. _____
4. _____
5. _____
6. _____

Stems

1. _____
2. _____
3. _____
4. _____
5. _____
6. _____

Leaves

1. _____
2. _____
3. _____
4. _____
5. _____
6. _____
7. _____

Fruit

1. _____
2. _____
3. _____
4. _____
5. _____
6. _____
7. _____

Seeds

1. _____
2. _____
3. _____
4. _____
5. _____
6. _____

Flower

1. _____
2. _____
3. _____
4. _____

4.6 Spice Hunt

Directions: *Work with a small group (3 to 5 students).* Your teacher
will have 12 numbered cups containing different spices.
With your group, bring three cups at a time to your table.
Try to identify the spices in the cups. Write the letter *and*
the name of each spice after the number of the cup on
the list below. *Check and discuss your answers with
the class.*

Cup

1. _____

2. _____

3. _____

4. _____

5. _____

6. _____

7. _____

8. _____

9. _____

10. _____

11. _____

12. _____

Spices

a. Cinnamon

b. Cumin

c. Cardamom

d. Nutmeg

e. Ginger

f. Cayenne pepper

g. Clove

h. Curry powder

i. Oregano

j. Black pepper

k. Mustard powder

l. Turmeric

4.7 The Nose Knows

Directions: *Work with a partner.* Your teacher will have ten
numbered, covered jars. Smell the contents of each
jar and try to identify what's inside. No peeking! Write
your answers below. *Compare your answers with
those of your partner and the rest of the class.*

Lemons are number _____ .

Rubbing alcohol is number _____ .

Perfume is number _____ .

Ammonia is number _____ .

Cinnamon is number _____ .

Vanilla is number _____ .

Peppermint is number _____ .

Cheese is number _____ .

_____ is number _____ .

_____ is number _____ .

4.8 Pudding Me On

Directions: *Work with a partner first and then a small group (3 to 5 students).* Your teacher will have everything you need to make instant pudding. With your partner, list all of those things below.

With your group, decide what flavor of pudding to make. Collect that package and all the other items needed to prepare the pudding. Then appoint a different person to do each of these things: read the instructions on the package out loud; follow the instructions; spoon the pudding into eight paper cups; and pass out the pudding to eight other students. Each student should receive two different puddings to sample. While you are eating, answer the questions below. *Everyone shares in the clean up!*

What we need:

_____   _____

_____   _____

_____   _____

_____   _____

1. Which pudding did your group make? _____

2. Which pudding did you sample? _____

3. Which pudding do you like best? _____

4.9 Salad Daze

Directions: *Work with a small group (3 to 5 students).* Tomorrow you are going to make a salad in class. Today your group needs to list all the things needed to make a good salad and a good salad dressing. Write those ingredients below. Decide who in your group will bring in each ingredient and write his or her name next to that ingredient on the list. Your teacher will bring in large bowls, knives, cutting boards, paper plates, and plastic forks.

Salad Ingredients:

1. lettuce   Maria _____

2. _____

3. _____

4. _____

5. _____

6. _____

7. _____

8. _____

9. _____

10. _____

Salad Dressing Ingredients:

1. _____

2. _____

3. _____

4. _____

5. _____

Continued

Directions: *Work with the same group.* Today you are going to make your salad. Check off all the ingredients your group has brought. Is everything ready? Now write down step-by-step directions for making the salad.

1. <u>Wash our hands</u>

2. <u>Wash the vegetables</u>

3. _____

4. _____

5. _____

6. _____

7. _____

8. _____

9. _____

10. _____

11. _____

4.10 Safety First!

Directions: *Work with a small group (4 to 5 students).* Your teacher will have ten numbered household items in class. Bring the items to your table two at a time. Use them to fill in information on the chart below. You may smell the items-- carefully!—but *do not taste them.* Some of these items can be dangerous if used incorrectly and all of them should be kept away from small children. *Share your answers with the class.*

Brand Name	Item	Where to Keep It	Used For
1. Parsons	ammonia	high shelf or locked cupboard in kitchen	cleaning
2.			
3.			
4.			
5.			
6.			
7.			
8.			
9.			
10.			

Purple Cows & Potato Chips ©1995 by Alta Book Center Publishers
Permission is granted to reproduce this page for classroom use.

4.11 Name the Perfume

Directions: *Work with a small group (3 students).* Your teacher will have ten numbered bottles of perfume in class. With your group, smell each fragrance and try to invent an appropriate name for it. Think of who might wear the fragrance. Write your answers below. *Share your answers with the class.*

Name of Perfume	Who Wears It
1.	
2.	
3.	
4.	
5.	
6.	
7.	
8.	
9.	
10.	

4.12 Taste Test

Directions: *Work alone.* Your teacher will have several numbered containers of different cola drinks and some paper cups in class. Pour yourself a small amount of each cola and taste it. Try to identify each cola by number on the list below. Then answer the questions and *compare your answers with those of the class.*

Classic Coke is number _____.

New Coke is number _____.

Cherry Coke is number _____.

Pepsi Cola is number _____.

Dr. Pepper is number _____.

1. How many colas did you guess correctly? _____

2. All the colas are the same color and all are carbonated. How can you tell the

   difference? _____

   _____

   _____

3. Which one do you like best? _____

   _____

   _____

4.13 Popcorn Popping

Directions: *Work with a partner.* Your teacher will bring in all of the items you need to make popcorn. Look at the items carefully and discuss with your partner the best way to use them to make popcorn. Then write down, in order, the different steps you must follow and compare your list to your partner's. *Share your list with the class.*

1. _____

2. _____

3. _____

4. _____

5. _____

6. _____

7. _____

8. _____

9. _____

10. _____

11. _____

12. _____

4.14 Lemon Aid

Directions: *Work with a small group (3 to 4 students).* Your teacher will bring some cut lemons to class. Take enough pieces for your group and pass them around. Describe how the lemon smells; then describe how it tastes. With your group, write down all of the things you have eaten or used that contained lemon or had lemon flavoring. See how many things you can think of. *Share your ideas with the class.*

It smells . . .

1. _____

2. _____

3. _____

4. _____

5. _____

It tastes . . .

1. _____

2. _____

3. _____

4. _____

5. _____

Things made with lemon:

1. _____

2. _____

3. _____

4. _____

5. _____

6. _____

7. _____

8. _____